MYSTERY STATES SERIES

SOUTHEAST REGION

Grades 4–5

Project Managers:
Thad H. McLaurin and Jennifer Munnerlyn

Writers:
Jan Brennan and Mary Sanford

Art Coordinator:
Barry Slate

Artists:
Clevell Harris, Sheila Krill, Mary Lester, Kimberly Richard,
Greg D. Rieves, Barry Slate

Cover Artist:
Clevell Harris

www.themailbox.com

©2001 by THE EDUCATION CENTER, INC.
All rights reserved.
ISBN #1-56234-449-8

Manufactured in the United States

10 9 8 7 6 5 4 3 2 1

Table of Contents

About This Book

Welcome to the Mystery States Series

Through active participation and investigation, the Mystery States series challenges your students to work collaboratively while learning about each of the five U.S. regions. This five-book series supplements and enhances your curriculum and provides a fun, creative, engaging way to teach your students about the U.S. regions. Each book contains a complete social studies investigation of a different region: Northeast, Southeast, Middle West, Southwest, West. Students work in cooperative groups gathering facts and information to form an investigation file to use in identifying a mystery state within each book's region. For ease of use, each book is divided into the following six sections:

- **Teacher's Guide**—Teachers are given detailed, step-by-step instructions on how to use and implement each part of the book.

- **Part 1: Discovering the Mystery State**—Students are introduced, through an original read-aloud, to a family living in the specified region. Using clues embedded in the story and provided clue cards, students work in groups to build an investigation file and identify the state in which the family lives—the mystery state.

- **Part 2: Investigating the Mystery State & Beyond**—Students investigate and research the identified mystery state by completing individual and small-group projects which involve students in a variety of social studies skills. Students also begin to learn more about other states within the region.

- **Part 3: Individual Regional Projects**—Each section contains 20 independent regional projects. These projects are designed to meet the needs of the various learning styles of students. This section also includes a contract for students to complete regarding the plans and completion dates of the selected projects. Also included is an assessment rubric for the teacher to use in evaluating the completed projects.

- **Part 4: Maps & Resources**—Each section contains related state, regional, and U.S. maps; patterns; and resource lists for literature, reference books, Web sites, and other contacts.

- **Part 5: Answer Keys & Checklist**—Each section contains a detailed answer key as well as a reproducible checklist that a teacher can use to keep track of each activity completed by each student.

Benefits of the Mystery States Series:
- Supports national social studies standards developed by the National Council for the Social Studies (NCSS)
- Supplements and enhances fourth- and fifth-grade social studies curricula
- Contains a step-by-step teacher's guide
- Encourages active involvement through independent and small-group activities
- Requires higher-order thinking skills and targets different learning styles
- Promotes students' success

Teacher's Guide

Part 1: Discovering the Mystery State

Part 1 is designed to be completed in the step-by-step order presented below. In this section, students are introduced to a family living in a mystery state within the Southeast region through a read-aloud story. Students work in small groups to uncover clues embedded in the story as well as complete other activities in which they work in collaborative groups researching, interpreting, and analyzing information to help them predict the mystery state's identity.

Step 1: Have 12 different students, in turn, locate one of these states on a U.S. wall map: Alabama, Arkansas, Florida, Georgia, Kentucky, Louisiana, Mississippi, North Carolina, South Carolina, Tennessee, Virginia, and West Virginia. Inform your students that they've just identified the states of the Southeast region.

Step 2: Divide students into six groups. Give each group a copy of "Grounded" (pages 8–14). Also, give each student one copy of "Investigation File" (page 15), "Investigation State Checklist" (page 17), the regional and U.S. maps (pages 39 and 40), and a file folder. (Have students keep all reproducibles and gathered research in the file folder throughout the investigation.) Instruct the students in each group to label each Southeast state on their regional maps (page 39). Then direct the students to use a red crayon or colored pencil to shade in the Southeast region on their U.S. maps (page 40).

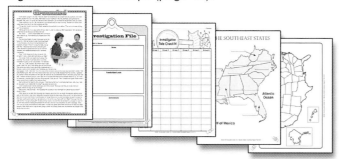

Step 3: Tell students that they are about to become super sleuths in an investigation of the Southeast region. Explain that you're going to read aloud a story about a family who lives in a state within the Southeast region. Direct students to listen carefully as you read the story. Next, tell your students that you're going to read the story a second time, but this time each student is to jot down on the "Investigation File" (page 15) any clues that the story reveals about the state in which the family lives. Remind students to listen for clues, such as geographic references, climate/weather information, and references to occupations, food, plants, and/or animals.

Step 4: After reading the story, allow time for students to compare notes within their groups. Then have a representative from each group read aloud the clues her group discovered. Encourage each group to add to its notes any clues not listed. Have each group evaluate the revised clues and then list in the "Possibilities/Leads" section of page 15 any states in which they think Collin's family might live.

Step 5: Make a copy of page 16; then cut the reproducible into six separate clue cards. Distribute one clue card to each group and inform the group it has several clues to research that will help bring the class closer to the mystery state's identity. Provide ample time for each group to research its clues. Make available a variety of regional references as well as almanacs, encyclopedias, and atlases. (For a list of resources, see page 42.)

Step 6: Hold a conference with each group once it has answered its clues. If the answers are incorrect, guide the group toward finding the correct answers.

Step 7: Have a member of each group read aloud her group's clues and answers. Instruct each student to record each group's clues and answers on the back of her "Investigation File" for future reference.

Step 8: Have each group use the "Investigation State Checklist" (page 17) to check off any states that could possibly be Collin's home based on the gathered clues and clue card information. Then have each group read aloud the states it checked as the other groups record the information in the appropriate columns on their checklists.

Step 9: Instruct each group to use the checklist to eliminate any states not considered as the mystery state and record those states at the bottom of page 15. Then have the group use the checklist information to help it predict the mystery state's identity. After coming to a consensus, have each group member write her prediction on the back of the checklist.

Step 10: Give each student one copy of "Crack the Code" (page 18). Have the student find out the mystery state's identity by completing the reproducible as directed. Take a poll to see how many groups made correct predictions.

Part 2: Investigating the Mystery State & Beyond

The five activities in this section are designed to be completed in any order. Also, the activities are independent of one another so you can select the activities that best fit your students' needs. Each activity can be completed individually, in pairs, or in small groups.

North Carolina on My Mind (Pages 20–22)
(Research, Writing)

By completing this activity, students will become more familiar with the mystery state—North Carolina. Students are challenged to research topics related to North Carolina, such as location, land features, natural resources, climate and weather, Native Americans, and more.

Materials for each student or group of students: 1 copy each of pages 20, 21, and 22; access to references on North Carolina and the Southeast region

Directions: Make available various resources on North Carolina and the Southeast region (see resource list on page 42). After students research the various topics and take notes, have them write complete sentences about each topic in the appropriate sections of pages 20, 21, and 22. If desired, gather the completed work and staple each set of reproducibles along the top, creating a flip booklet. Post each booklet on a bulletin board titled "North Carolina on My Mind." Enlarge, cut out, and color the North Carolina symbols on page 41 and post them around the display. As an extension activity, have students work in pairs or small groups to research the 11 other Southeast states, using the same topics listed on pages 20 through 22. This will provide excellent information students can use to compare the 12 Southeast states.

The Lost Colony (Pages 23–24)
(Research, Writing)

This activity has students researching the Lost Colony of North Carolina and presenting their findings at an archaeological association meeting.

Materials for each student or group of students: 1 copy of pages 23 and 24; various reference materials on the Lost Colony, North Carolina, and archaeologists; crayons or markers; glue; file folder

Directions: In advance, make a copy of page 24; then program the Lost Colony Archaeological Association invitation at the bottom of the page with the desired group members' names (three to four students per group), date, and time. Next, make one copy of the programmed sheet for each group. To begin the activity, explain to students that they are groups of archaeologists researching the Lost Colony and will be presenting their findings to the class. Direct students to complete page 23 and the top of page 24 as directed. Have each group display its completed work in a file folder as shown. Then have each group present its findings to the class on the appointed day and time.

Guess Who (Pages 25–27)
(Researching a Notable Person, Writing)

This activity will allow students to research notable persons from North Carolina, such as actors, writers, and scientists.

Materials for each student or group of students: 1 copy of page 25, 1 illustration from page 26 or 27, glue, scissors

Directions: In advance, make two or three copies of each illustration on pages 26 and 27. Next, assign each student or group of students one of the notable persons from pages 26 and 27. Supply each student or group with the materials listed. Then direct students to complete page 25 by using encyclopedias and various other reference materials. Inform students not to use the person's name anywhere on the front of page 25. Once students complete page 25, have them cut the flap as shown and glue the illustration on the back of page 25 so it shows through the flap. Display students' work on a bulletin board titled "Who's Who Gallery." Tack one 9" x 12" sheet of construction paper on the board for each student or group. Then mount each "Guess Who" page to one of the sheets of construction paper by stapling along the edges of the reproducible. Encourage students to visit the board, read a "Guess Who" page, guess the identity of the notable person, and then lift the flap to reveal the answer.

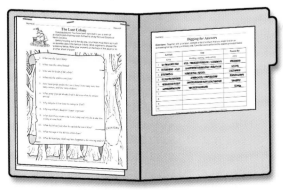

Hurricane Lab (Pages 28–29)
(Research)

This activity has students working for a hurricane lab to help inform others about the dangers of hurricanes.

Materials for each student or group of students: 1 copy of pages 28 and 29, access to reference materials on North Carolina and the Southeast, poster board, a variety of art supplies, markers or crayons

Directions: Make available various resources on North Carolina and the Southeast (see resource list on page 42). After students complete page 28, have them use the poster board and art supplies to create an informational poster about the dangers of hurricanes. Display the posters around your room or school to make others aware of hurricane dangers. Then have students practice plotting the movement of a hurricane by completing page 29.

Separate…But Equal? (Page 30)
(Research, Writing)

This activity will allow students to reserach some important people who were active participants during the Southeast's struggle for civil rights.

Materials for each student or group of students: 1 copy of page 30, access to reference materials on civil rights and the Southeast, 2 sheets of 8½" x 11" colored construction paper, a variety of art supplies, markers or crayons

Directions: Make available various resources on civil rights and the Southeast (see resource list on page 42). Divide students into groups of four; then have each group member complete page 30 as directed. After each group completes its research, select one group member to staple the group's research papers between the two construction paper covers. Direct the student to use the art supplies to decorate her group's cover and title it "Separate…But Equal."

Beyond the Borders of North Carolina (Pages 31–32)
(Mapmaking, Research)

This mapmaking activity takes students beyond the borders of North Carolina to learn more about the 11 other states in the Southeast region.

Materials for each student or group of students: 1 copy of page 31, 1 enlarged copy of page 32 on an 11" x 14" sheet of paper, crayons or colored pencils

Directions: Provide each student or group of students with the materials listed. Also make available various reference materials on the Southeast region (see resource list on page 42). Instruct each student or group of students to complete pages 31 and 32 as directed. If desired, place an enlarged outline map of the Southeast region (see map on page 39) labeled with the appropriate state names in the center of a bulletin board. Arrange the student-created maps around the enlarged map. Title the display "Beyond the Borders of North Carolina."

Part 3: Individual Regional Projects

The research topics, contracts, and rubric in this section are designed to provide each student with an opportunity to successfully complete research on the Southeast region. The projects are grouped into four quadrants according to different learning styles.

Pick-a-Project (Pages 34–36)
(Research)

Materials for each student: 1 copy each of pages 34, 35, and 36; access to various reference materials on the Southeast region; a variety of art supplies

Directions:

Step 1: Assign each student (or allow her to choose) one or more projects from one or more quadrants on page 34.

Step 2: Provide each student with a copy of the "Pick-a-Project Contract" (page 35). After discussing due dates and other pertinent information, direct each student to complete the contract(s) and sign at the bottom. After reviewing each student's contract, add your signature at the bottom.

Step 3: Provide each student with a copy of the "Pick-a-Project Rubric" (page 36). Discuss the grading criteria on the rubric with your students. After a student completes each assigned project, use the rubric to evaluate her project. (Page 36 can be used to evaluate up to four projects per student.) Using the rubric will help you evaluate each student's project(s) on eight different criteria, using a scale of 1 to 5 (1 = Poor, 3 = Good, 5 = Outstanding).

Part 4: Maps & Resources

Part 4 contains related state, regional, and U.S. maps; symbols; and resource lists for related literature and reference books, Web sites, and other contacts. Many of the maps and resources are used in conjunction with the activities in Part 1 and Part 2.

- North Carolina Outline Map (page 38)
- The Southeast States (page 39)
- The United States (page 40)
- Symbols of North Carolina (page 41)
- Resource Guide (page 42)

Part 5: Answer Keys & Checklist

Part 5 contains a detailed answer key as well as a reproducible checklist that you can use to keep track of each activity completed by each student.

PART 1: DISCOVERING THE MYSTERY STATE

Collin bolted upright in his bed. "Get out, Dad!" he screamed as he jumped from his top bunk. His crash landing startled him out of his sleep. He looked around frightfully in the inky darkness and gathered his thoughts. "Oh, man, I've got to tell Dad about that nightmare!" he mumbled as he stumbled back up to bed.

"Rise and shine, my son," Mr. Henderson commanded early the next morning. "Shower and dress; then come down for a bite to eat. We're leaving at 0700."

"I'll rise, but I doubt I can shine," Collin replied as he perched on one elbow. "The sun's not even shining yet," he complained.

"We've got to be on our way before the sun rises in order to make our 0800 reservation," Mr. Henderson called back as he disappeared down the hall.

"But, Dad, I…" Collin's voice trailed off to a whisper, "don't want to go," he finished as he flopped back onto his pillow.

The soothing fingers of water massaged some life back into Collin as he stood under the showerhead. "I'll tell Dad about my dream during breakfast," he mused to himself. "There's no way he'll take me up after that." Resolved that he had a fail-safe plan, Collin whistled a lighthearted tune as he dried off, dressed, and headed downstairs full of renewed confidence.

"Dad," Collin began as he dug his spoon into his grits, "I had a dream last night about our flight."

"You know, Collin, you seem much calmer this morning. Your dream must have shown you how incredible it's going to be!" Dad smiled. "I'm relieved."

"Ah…no," Collin retorted. "My dream was a nightmare! Listen! You and I were flying right into a hurricane. The plane was being thrown about like a helpless leaf in a tornado. I felt so sick I wanted to die. Suddenly you turned to me and gasped, 'Collin, take over.' Your face was white and pasty; your entire body was drenched in sweat. Your eyes flashed panic, then shut. Your head rocked back and your hands dropped from the controls. I grabbed my copilot's wheel and jerked it to the right. We went into an uncontrollable tailspin and were going down real fast. I realized we were going to crash right into a mountain that was looming straight ahead of us, so I tried to rouse you. I pushed open your door and screamed, 'Dad, get out!' Then I jumped out myself. That's when I woke up and found myself on my bedroom floor."

Dad scratched his head in utter confusion. "After having had such a terrifying nightmare, why, may I ask, do you seem much calmer this morning?" he asked incredulously.

Collin looked straight into his dad's eyes and firmly stated, "Because now that you know what can happen, there's no way we can fly today!"

Dad couldn't help but laugh. "You're basing the success of your first flight on a three-second dream? Really, Collin!"

Collin glared at his dad, then shoveled two heaping spoonfuls into his mouth. Accidentally spilling some grits on his mother's new cotton tablecloth, he angrily wiped the stain away. Why couldn't his dad accept the fact that not everyone shared his enthusiasm for flying? Ever since his dad had gotten his pilot's license he had been pushing and pushing to get everyone in the family to go flying with him. Wasn't it enough that his older brother had gone flying with his dad and had loved it so much that he enrolled in a program to learn to fly, too? But instead of taking the pressure off of Collin, that had only intensified his dad's campaign. "Why can't you be brave and adventurous like Pete?" his dad had jeered when Pete announced his desire to take lessons. Well, there was no way he was going to climb into a flying death trap just because two people in his family had no brains.

Collin finished his breakfast in silence. He hadn't even looked at his dad since he had so rudely joked about his nightmare. Mr. Henderson finally broke the silence.

"Look, Collin, I'm sorry I laughed at you. It's just that…" He searched for the appropriate words. "All your fears…," he paused again. "I really believe that if you'd give it one try, you'd see what has hooked me." He gave Collin a minute to think, then continued. "Have you ever known me to be reckless or risk-taking? Gosh, Collin, I even wore seat belts before they were required by law! How many of your friends are NASCAR® fans? I think car racing is far more dangerous than flying." Collin remained silent and unmoved. Mr. Henderson continued, "Haven't you ever looked at a bird in flight and wished you could be that free? Aren't you the least bit curious about what the world looks like from above? It's so incredible; I can't put it into words. Collin, I just want you to see that world."

Collin considered all that his dad had said. "Yeah, sure, that all sounds great. But Dad, you've got to admit, there are certain dangers in flying."

"Sure, but there are dangers in crossing the street, too! But before you cross, you stop, look, and listen. And before I fly I take every precaution to ensure a safe flight. For example, I never fly if there is a storm predicted where I'm taking off or where I plan to land. I always check the radar at the airport an hour before my flight. So we'd never find ourselves flying right into a storm like in your dream. Another precaution I've summed up with this rhyme: 'Never take a flight if you don't feel right.' I never fly if I'm not feeling absolutely terrific. I promise I won't turn ghastly white and pass out on you! And as far as the mountains are concerned, we can take an easterly route so that we stay completely away from them."

"But when Pete went up with you he told me he sat at his own set of controls just in case he needed to take over for you. I'm only 12 years old—I don't want to do that!" Collin admitted.

"I promise you won't have to," Dad replied. Collin still didn't look convinced, so Mr. Henderson added, "If you'd feel better, I can ask Joe to join us as copilot. I'll upgrade our reservation and take a Cessna® 172—a four seater—so that you can relax in the backseat." Collin knew Joe was certainly a competent copilot—he had been his dad's instructor.

"Do you think I'll get sick?" Collin asked.

"No, but if you want, you can take some medication an hour before the flight as a precaution," Dad offered.

Collin spoke slowly. "I can't think of any more excuses."

Mr. Henderson's face brightened. "Then, let's do it!" he cheered. They high-fived each other as Dad promised, "You'll love it. I just know you will!"

Mr. Henderson pulled into the airport parking lot at 0730. He gathered up his equipment: his portable GPS (Global Positioning System), two headsets, and his flight bag.

"Okay, first we'll check in with Jennifer at the front desk. Then we'll look at the radar for the latest weather report. If all looks clear, I'll take you over to our reserved plane and we'll start our preflight preparations," he said with enthusiasm.

"When will Joe get here?" Collin asked.

"He said he'd meet us at the plane by 0800," Dad said. "Don't worry, Collin, you can count on Joe to be here on time," Mr. Henderson added reassuringly. He walked up to the desk.

"Good morning, Jennifer. I'd like you to meet my son, Collin," Mr. Henderson said.

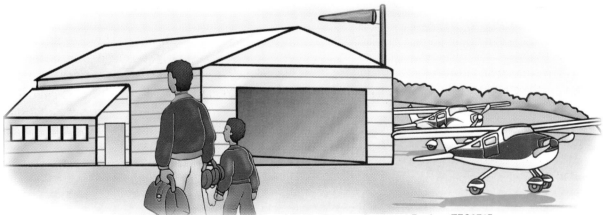

"Well, it's certainly nice to meet you, Collin," Jennifer replied as she extended her hand to him. "I understand this is your maiden voyage, so to speak. Well, your dad couldn't have picked a better day to fly. There's not a cloud in the sky and not a storm in sight! And, you know, this is the best time of day to fly; mornings are the calmest." She turned to Mr. Henderson and added, "Who knows? Perhaps you'll have another student pilot on your hands, Tom!"

Collin laughed nervously, "Let's not rush things!"

"One step at a time!" Mr. Henderson soothed. "Jennifer, when Joe checks in tell him we're out readying the plane, okay?"

"You bet," she answered. "I expect him back soon. Have a great flight, guys. And Collin, stop by later and tell me all about it."

Collin nodded in reply; then he and his dad did a quick radar check to confirm Jennifer's weather report. It was definitely a great day for a flight! Collin followed his dad out to the hangar to find their plane. As he walked amongst the two-seater and four-seater planes, he couldn't help but notice how tiny and frail the planes all looked. He couldn't believe he was actually going to sit in something that fragile—that puny—and soar thousands of feet up in the air at speeds he really didn't care to think about.

"Here she is, Collin. What do you think?" his dad called out as he placed his equipment next to one of the four-seater Cessnas®. Collin walked over to the plane and circled around it slowly. It sure looked different from the commercial planes he was used to seeing. It looked more like an overgrown dragonfly! The wings were on top and the wheels were encased in what looked like large white booties to match the body of the plane.

"I don't know, Dad. It's even smaller than I pictured," Collin said nervously.

"It's bigger on the inside than many cars on the road today," his dad replied. "Don't worry so much. Here, help me with the preflight inspection," he added, hoping to divert Collin's attention.

Mr. Henderson showed Collin how to check the various gauges; manually check the rudder, aileron, and wing flaps; and check for fuel. "It looks like we need to top off the tank. Collin, use this phone to call Jennifer and ask her to send the gas attendant over," he said to Collin as he handed him the portable phone. Within minutes the plane was being filled, much to Collin's surprise, at the top of the wings. "The gas tanks are in the wings?" he asked his dad.

"Yep, each wing holds 25 gallons," he answered as he handed Collin a small, clear plastic cylinder. "Watch me as I check the gas for its purity, then you can check the other wing." Mr. Henderson inserted a needle that was in the center of the cylinder into a bubble on the wing and extracted a tiny amount of very light blue liquid. "Aviation gasoline has a bluish tint to it and must be pure," he explained. "This looks good," he surmised. "There are five spots to check on each wing. Once checked, you can carefully place the gas back in the tank," he said as he handed the cylinder to Collin.

"Hey, Dad, when is Joe getting here?" Collin asked after finishing the gas check.

"Let's see," Mr. Henderson replied as he checked his watch, "It's almost 0800. Real soon, I would guess, real soon."

Fifteen minutes later Collin and his dad had the plane 100 percent ready for takeoff but Joe was nowhere in sight. Mr. Henderson looked at his watch again. "Joe is always so punctual; I can't imagine what could've happened. Let me call Jennifer to see if she knows anything."

Collin circled the plane several times while his dad talked to Jennifer. He was still in awe that this birdlike structure was going to take him up and away! Suddenly Collin's dad approached him, handed him a headset and a pair of binoculars, and said, "Climb in, Collin. There's no time for questions—we've got to go now!" Collin saw the resolve in his father's eyes, the determination in his face and the tension in his body. He had a million questions and even more concerns, but decided this was not the time to ask. He followed his dad's every command. As he took his place in the copilot's seat, a twang of panic struck, but he forced it down by reassuring himself that his dad desperately needed him there. He fastened his seat belt, hooked up his headset, and adjusted it so he could communicate with his dad and hear his dad's communications with the control tower. A new sense of pride started to surface as Collin witnessed his dad—the pilot—take charge of

this emergency-like situation. After he methodically and meticulously completed a final check on all the gauges, Mr. Henderson shouted out the window, "CLEAR!" and then turned the key to start the engine. The noise that exploded from the propellers was numbing, but with his headset on, Collin could still hear his dad's voice. As they taxied out to the runway, Collin's dad finally filled him in.

"Joe is missing. Apparently he took off this morning at 0700 in an ultralight that the airport just acquired. He has been fine-tuning it for the past few days and thought this morning would be a great time to give it a test-flight. He was due back at 0730; Jennifer fears he has run into some kind of trouble."

"So, we're on a rescue mission?" Collin asked cautiously.

"No, it's more like a spotting mission," his dad replied. "We can't land like a helicopter. But we can try to spot him, and when we do, we'll use our GPS to determine the exact coordinates of his location. Then we can radio that information back to Jennifer so she can send help by land."

"Okay, Dad, just tell me what you need me to do," Collin announced as the adrenaline coursed through his body.

"For now, just sit back and prepare for takeoff, Collin. We'll be heading south into the wind."

Collin gripped the edges of his seat and pushed his head back against the headrest. He took several deep breaths to try to squelch the butterflies in his stomach, then glanced over at his dad. They exchanged a silent but powerful thumbs-up. After receiving their final clearance from the control tower, they were on their way. The takeoff was fast; the climb was exhilarating. Collin closed his eyes and felt the warm wind whipping across his face. He listened to the thunderous roar of the engine and felt its throb vibrating through his body.

"Collin, are you okay?" His dad's voice gently rocked him back to reality.

"Oh, yeah, Dad. This isn't so bad!" he confessed.

"That's great, Collin. I need you now," his dad continued. "Your job is to use the binoculars and look all around to try and spot Joe. The ultralight that he was flying should be pretty easy to see—it has a bright yellow and purple sail. I'll fly as low as I can to give us the best possible view. It's a perfectly clear day, so that's in our favor, too."

Collin readied his binoculars and glanced out his window. He was amazed at the view below. He always knew there were a lot of trees where he lived, but from above, they seemed to dominate the land. He spied a few twisty slivers of space that had chiseled little grooves between the green here and there. His eyes followed one of the larger roads and saw that it led to an open space.

"Hey, Dad, doesn't Salem look small from up here?" he asked.

"It sure does," he answered. "What do you think of your hometown now?"

"It's amazing!" Collin exclaimed. "Everything looks totally different. It doesn't even look like anybody lives down there."

"Well, let's hope we can find one somebody down there," his dad reminded him. "Keep your eyes out for Joe now. We've been up for almost ten minutes, so we've covered about 15 miles. Assuming the wind direction hasn't changed and Joe was traveling approximately the same course, we might be able to spot the yellow and purple sail any time now."

Collin kept his eyes fixed on the terrain below. He saw endless rows of leafy green tobacco, neighborhoods of gray rooftops, and a midnight blue lake, but no yellow and purple ultralight.

After flying south for about ten more minutes, Mr. Henderson decided to change directions. "I think we need to broaden our search; I'm going to head east and fly in the direction of the coast," he told Collin. "Keep your binoculars focused."

Collin took a deep breath and sighed. What if Joe had gone down in the ocean? His mind started to race with so many new questions and fears, but he didn't want to give in to them. He remained silent and concentrated on his task.

They flew on in silence for what seemed like hours. Mr. Henderson focused on the course and altered the direction several times. He used his portable GPS to keep track of where they were and updated Collin by pointing out various landmarks. Every ten minutes or so he communicated with the control tower to see if anyone had any news about Joe, but still there was nothing.

"Dad, how long can we fly on a full tank of gas?" Collin's voice shot out above the drone of the engine.

"Fortunately, that is one of our least concerns, Collin. We started with a full tank, which is 50 gallons, and we burn about eight gallons an hour, so we can fly for around six hours. But, I'm starting to think that even if we were up here for six hours, we probably wouldn't find Joe. Maybe he has had enough time to pack up the sail, and without that to look for, it would be like last autumn when we spent three hours looking for your mother's lost ring in the mounds of fall leaves. I think we should head back."

"But, Dad, we found Mom's ring; we didn't give up until we did. Do you really think we should give up on Joe?"

"The difference is that we knew Mom's ring was somewhere in the leaves. She had it on when she started raking. We don't know for sure that Joe is still out here somewhere," Collin's dad explained.

"But wouldn't he have contacted someone by now if he was okay?" Collin asked.

"It sure seems like he would have," his dad replied. "I can't figure it out. Joe is a very responsible man and a very cautious flier. The pieces of the puzzle just don't fit."

Collin continued his investigative questioning. "How long has it been since Joe took off this morning?"

"He left at 0700 and it is now 0900," his dad replied. "But remember, he was scheduled to land at 0730, so he must have had trouble within those first 30 minutes."

"And how far could an ultralight go in half an hour?" Collin asked.

"I'd estimate about 30 miles since an ultralight flies at around 60 miles per hour."

"Have we covered that 30-mile radius in all directions?" Collin asked.

"Not completely," his dad answered thoughtfully. "Let's head back, Collin, but as we go we'll circle around toward the north and even the west, if necessary. Perhaps the wind shifted and Joe was forced to fly off course."

Mr. Henderson banked the plane to the left and headed north with a renewed sense of hope. Collin sat up straighter in his seat and scanned the land below. How he prayed he would see some yellow and purple somewhere soon.

They flew on in total concentration for awhile. Mr. Henderson was checking in with the control tower again when Collin thought he saw a splash of color.

"Dad," his voice shot out powerfully. "Out my window—to the north—I think I see something in the distance. Can we fly lower?"

Mr. Henderson immediately pulled back on the throttle and pushed forward on the yoke, lowering the plane. Collin glanced at the altimeter and saw the needle level off at 1000 feet. He kept his eyes fixed on the spot where he had seen something and sure enough, as they got closer to it, it was definitely something yellow and purple. Mr. Henderson saw it, too.

"Collin, I think we've found him! Now listen," he continued. "There are two critical things we must do right now. First, we need to be absolutely sure of the coordinates on the GPS so I can radio that information back, and second, we need to look as closely as we can to see if there is any movement down there. If Joe has been down this long with no communication attempt, he may be in very bad shape."

While Collin focused his binoculars on the spot, Mr. Henderson readied the GPS. He noted the coordinates as they flew directly overhead and immediately radioed them in. Collin focused on the sail even after they passed over, trying to will some movement, but he saw none.

Almost afraid to ask, Collin quietly said, "Dad, do you think Joe is alive?"

"I don't want to speculate on that," his dad uttered. "All we can do now is pray for him and head back to wait for an answer. Sit tight and we'll be landing in about 15 minutes."

For the next 15 minutes Collin's head swam with various scenarios of what could have happened to Joe. He pictured the ultralight crashing to the ground; he saw Joe lying unconscious under the sail; he imagined the rescue team finding Joe and attempting to resuscitate him. These visions crowded his brain until his dad signaled that they were about to land. Collin took a deep breath and prepared for this final portion of the ride. He decided to close his eyes and entrust a smooth landing to his dad. He felt the plane make a decisive deceleration, followed by a moment of what seemed like nonmovement. Then all of a sudden he felt the surge of power as the tires touched down and gradually braked to a complete stop. Collin opened his eyes to

find that they had taxied right over to the hangar where this whole journey had begun. Although he was relieved to have returned safely to the earth, he didn't feel the total peace he had originally expected. He desperately wanted to know how Joe was. He turned to his dad and asked, "Can we stay around to find out about Joe?"

"Absolutely," Mr. Henderson replied as he opened his pilot's door. "Hop out and we'll go inside to see if anyone has any information yet. We can come back to secure the plane later."

Father and son hurried over to the office and apprehensively approached Jennifer.

"Any news about Joe yet?" Mr. Henderson asked.

"Yes," she replied. "The rescue team radioed us twenty minutes ago. They found him conscious but quite disoriented. They fear several broken bones—definitely both legs, perhaps an arm, and probably several ribs. He must have had a concussion, too, but they are bringing him to the hospital as we speak and feel in time he will be fine."

Mr. Henderson asked further, "Does anyone know what happened?"

Jennifer speculated, "Joe had been rebuilding the engine on this ultralight for the past few days. I know how meticulous he is, but perhaps he missed something. A loose bolt, a missing safety ring, even a dirty belt could be enough to force a landing. We have a team that is retrieving the ultralight now. They'll do a thorough investigation to find the cause so that we can all learn from this near disaster."

Collin was listening intently to every word. He couldn't believe all that had happened and was about to ask his dad a question when something caught his eye. An ambulance had just pulled up and was parking right outside the office. An attendant got out and rushed toward them. He explained, "Our patient won't allow us to take him to the hospital until he speaks with a man by the name of Tom Henderson. Do you know him?"

Mr. Henderson stepped forward. "I'm Tom Henderson."

"Come with me, please," the attendant stated.

Jennifer and Collin followed his dad outside, fearing what they'd see or hear. The attendant guided them over to the back of the ambulance where Mr. Henderson anxiously stepped inside to see Joe. Joe wearily looked up from the stretcher and tried to extend his arm to shake hands with Mr. Henderson.

"Oh, sorry, Tom, I forgot," he said in a thin, pained voice. "I guess I can't raise my arm that high right now."

"Joe, what are you doing?" Mr. Henderson asked. "You've got to get to the hospital. They'll take good care of you and help ease your pain."

"Oh, I know that, Tom. But I wanted to thank you for saving my life! I understand that you were the one who spotted me. If it weren't for you I might have been there until I bled to death!"

"Joe…," Mr. Henderson paused, then said, "I'll be right back," and rushed out of the ambulance. He grabbed Collin's hand and said in his no-questions-asked kind of voice, "Come with me, son." They entered the back of the ambulance together, and as Mr. Henderson proudly put his arm around Collin he announced to Joe, "This is the young man to whom you owe your life. This is my son, Collin, who until today never wanted to set foot in an airplane. But when I needed him, he rose to the occasion and did everything in his power to find you. He didn't quit even when I said we should head back. It is Collin who deserves your thanks, Joe!"

Joe painfully raised his right hand to his forehead and saluted Collin. "Then it is to you I salute and owe my undying gratitude."

Collin felt a multitude of feelings welling up inside him as he humbly answered, "I'm just so relieved you're going to be okay, sir." He paused, then added, "And that we're all back on the ground!"

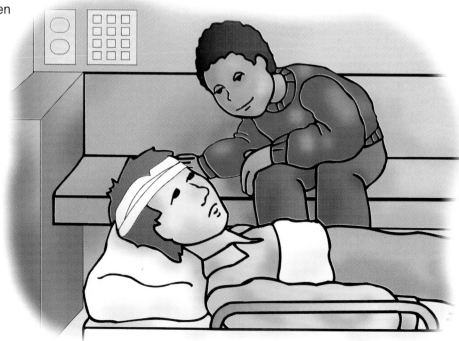

©2001 The Education Center, Inc. • *Mystery States* • Southeast Region • TEC3715

Investigation File

Investigator's Name: _____

Notes

Possibilities/Leads

Eliminations

15

Clue Cards

CLUE #1

Collin's family lived in the town of Salem.

1. Which states entirely east of the Mississippi River have a town named Salem?
2. Which of these states border the Atlantic ocean?

©2001 The Education Center, Inc.

CLUE #2

Collin feared flying into a hurricane.

1. What defines a storm as a hurricane?
2. Which states have been directly hit by a hurricane since 1900?
3. What four states have been most frequently hit by hurricanes since 1900?

©2001 The Education Center, Inc.

CLUE #3

Collin and his dad could have flown over both mountains and an ocean.

1. What states east of the Mississippi River have both mountains and an ocean coastline?
2. Which of these states lie below 40°N latitude?

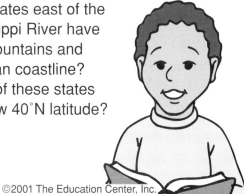

©2001 The Education Center, Inc.

CLUE #4

Mr. Henderson mentioned that some of Collin's friends were NASCAR® fans.

1. Which states located entirely below 40°N latitude and entirely east of 90°W longitude have NASCAR® tracks?
2. Which of these states are coastal states?

©2001 The Education Center, Inc.

CLUE #5

Collin spilled his grits on the cotton tablecloth.

1. Which states are leading producers of cotton?
2. Which of these states are located entirely between 75°W and 95°W longitude?
3. Which of these states (from number 2) are coastal states?

©2001 The Education Center, Inc.

CLUE #6

Collin spotted tobacco fields from up in the plane.

1. Which states located between 40°N and 30°N latitude are leading producers of tobacco?
2. Which of these states are coastal states?

©2001 The Education Center, Inc.

©2001 The Education Center, Inc. • *Mystery States* • *Southeast Region* • TEC3715 • Key p. 44

Name _____ Checklist

Investigation State Checklist

STATES	Group 1	Group 2	Group 3	Group 4	Group 5	Group 6
Alabama						
Arkansas						
Florida						
Georgia						
Kentucky						
Louisiana						
Mississippi						
North Carolina						
South Carolina						
Tennessee						
Virginia						
West Virginia						

©2001 The Education Center, Inc. • *Mystery States* • Southeast Region • TEC3715

17

Crack the Code

Directions: To discover the name and nickname of the mystery state, use the code box below to help you find a letter that matches each Morse code symbol. Write the corresponding letter in the blank beneath each symbol.

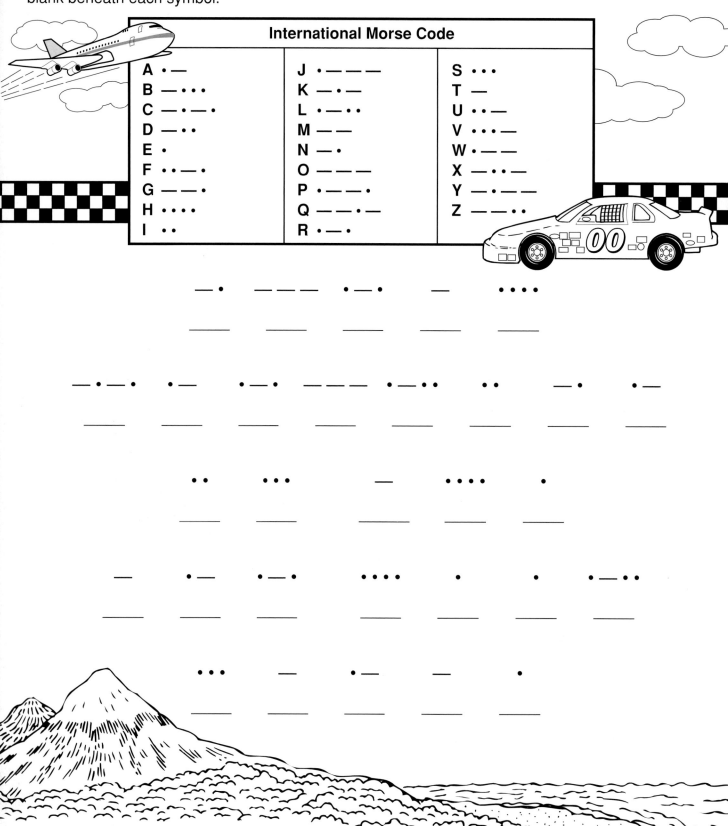

International Morse Code

A ·—	J ·———	S ···
B —···	K —·—	T —
C —·—·	L ·—··	U ··—
D —··	M ——	V ···—
E ·	N —·	W ·——
F ··—·	O ———	X —··—
G ——·	P ·——·	Y —·——
H ····	Q ——·—	Z ——··
I ··	R ·—·	

—·   ———   ·—·   —   ····
___ ___ ___ ___ ___

—·—·   ·—·   ·—·   ·——·   ··   —·   ·—
___ ___ ___ ___ ___ ___ ___

··   ···   —   ····   ·
___ ___ ___ ___ ___

—   ·—   ·—·   ····   ·   ·   ·—··
___ ___ ___ ___ ___ ___ ___

···   —   ·—   —   ·
___ ___ ___ ___ ___

PART 2: INVESTIGATING THE MYSTERY STATE & BEYOND

Name _____

20

North Carolina on My Mind

Physical Land Features

_____
_____
_____
_____
_____
_____

Natural Resources

_____
_____
_____
_____
_____
_____
_____

Climate & Weather

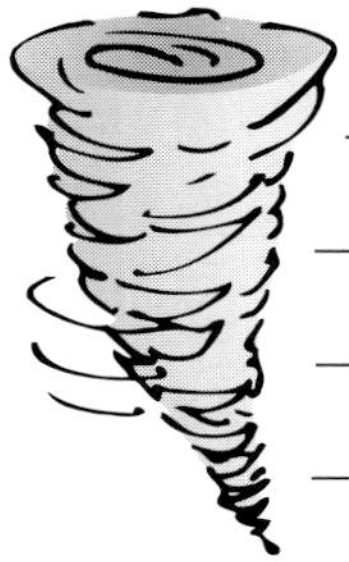

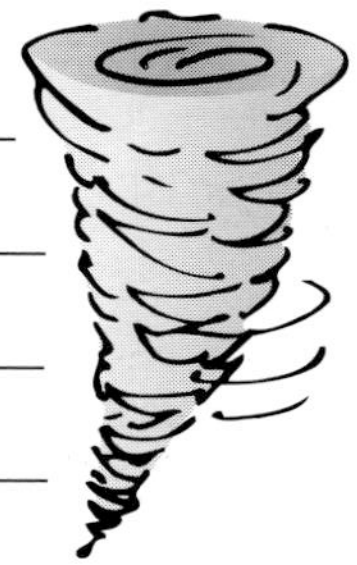

_____
_____
_____
_____
_____

State Capital: _____

State Tree: _____

State Flower: _____

State Bird: _____

Location

N

E

S

W

_____
_____
_____
_____
_____

Name _____

History

Famous Landmarks

Native Americans

Food

Famous People

21

Name

22

Plants

Animals

Inventions, Discoveries, & Firsts

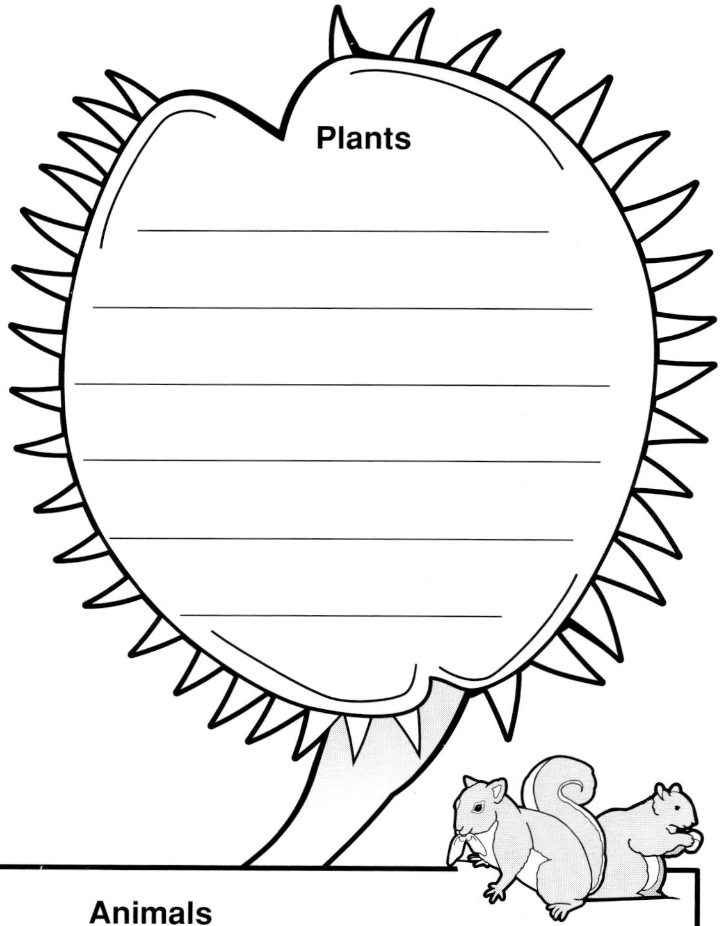

Economy

Places of Interest

Historic Location

The Lost Colony

Congratulations! You have been selected to join a team of archaeologists that has been formed to study the Lost Colony of North Carolina.

Before heading out to the dig site, your team must learn as much as possible about this famous colony. Work together to answer the questions below. Write your answers on the back of this page or on another sheet of paper.

1. What was the Lost Colony?

2. Where was the colony located?

3. Who was the leader of the colony?

4. Where did the settlers come from?

5. How many people settled the Lost Colony? How many men, how many women, and how many children?

6. What group of people already lived in the area when the settlers arrived?

7. Why did John White leave the colony in 1587?

8. Why was White's daughter Eleanor important?

9. When did White return to the Lost Colony and why did it take him so long to come back?

10. What did White find when he reached the Lost Colony?

11. What message or clue did the settlers leave?

12. What do historians think may have happened to the missing settlers?

CROATOAN

Name(s) ______________________________

Digging for Answers

Directions: Together with your team, compile a list of artifacts that you might find on an archaeological dig of the Lost Colony site. Describe each artifact in the spaces provided below.

Artifact	Use	Found By
Knife	Hunting, carving, and cutting	Joey
1.		
2.		
3.		
4.		
5.		
6.		
7.		
8.		
9.		
10.		

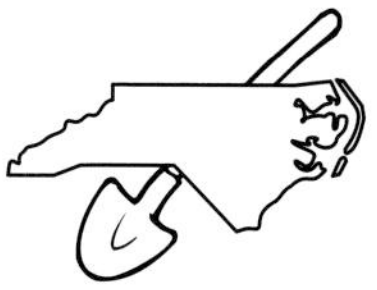

The Lost Colony Archaeological Association

invites you to

its annual conference.

Each team will present its findings.

We look forward to your expert presentation.

Group Members: ______________________________

Date: ______________________________

Time: ______________________________

©2001 The Education Center, Inc. • *Mystery States* • *Southeast Region* • TEC3715

Name(s) _____

Guess Who

Clue 1: Birthdate

_____

Clue 2:
Occupation/profession
for which this person
is most noted

_____
_____
_____
_____
_____

**Lift up this flap
to reveal the
identity of this
North Carolina
mystery person.**

Cut.

Fold.

Cut.

Cut.

Clue 3: Information that ties this person to the state of North Carolina

_____
_____

Clue 4: More specific details about this person and his/her accomplishments

_____
_____
_____
_____

Who's Who Gallery

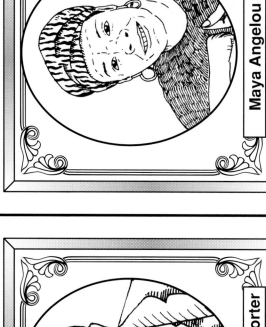

Maya Angelou

Charles Kuralt

William Sidney Porter

Thelonious Monk

Elizabeth Dole

Andy Griffith

©2001 The Education Center, Inc. • Mystery States • Southeast Region • TEC3715 • Key p. 45

Who's Who Gallery

Michael Jordan

Andrew Jackson

Richard Petty

Ava Gardner

Dolley Madison

Mia Hamm

Name(s)_____ *Research*

Hurricane Fast Facts

Almost every year North Carolina is threatened by hurricanes. These powerful storms can cause millions of dollars in damage. Hurricane labs want people to be better informed about the dangers of hurricanes. Help spread the word by researching hurricanes and answering the questions below.

1. Where do hurricanes form?

_____

2. What causes a hurricane to develop?

_____

3. How is a hurricane shaped?

_____

4. What is found in the middle of a hurricane?

_____

5. What is the range of a hurricane's possible wind speed?

_____

6. What makes a hurricane weaken?

_____

7. Across how many miles can the diameter of a hurricane stretch?

_____

8. What can meteorologists forecast about a hurricane?

_____

9. How far in advance are meteorologists able to issue warnings of a hurricane?

_____

10. How do hurricanes travel and at what rate?

_____

Name(s)_____

Hurricane Tracking

Pretend you are working for a hurricane lab. Use the lines of longitude and latitude shown on the map to chart Hurricane Gust's progress. Make a hurricane symbol (◎) to show the hurricane's location at each point.

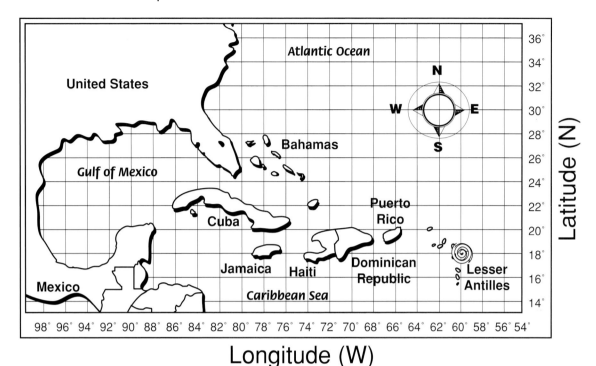

1. Hurricane Gust is spotted near the Lesser Antilles. (18°N, 60°W)

2. *Trade winds,* or large wind belts that blow toward the equator from the northeast or southeast, push Gust to the northwest. (21°N, 63°W)

3. Gust continues to move in a westerly direction. (21°N, 67°W)

4. Gust passes near the Dominican Republic and Haiti. (22°N, 70°W)

5. Winds push Gust northwest. (23°N, 75°W)

6. Passing through the Bahamas, Gust heads for Florida. (25°N, 78°W)

7. As Gust approaches the mainland, it continues north and travels along the coast. (28°N, 78°W)

8. Gust moves toward the coasts of Georgia and South Carolina. (31°N, 80°W)

9. North Carolina gets heavy rains, but Gust continues in a northeasterly fashion. (34°N, 80°W)

10. *Prevailing westerlies,* strong winds blowing around the earth from west to east, push Gust back out to sea! (36°N, 75°W)

Separate...But Equal?

Directions: Choose a person or event from below. Then write a report answering the questions *who, what, when, where,* and *why* about the person or the event. In your report use as many terms from the box at the bottom of the page that apply.

Martin Luther King Jr.	**North Carolina Sit-Ins**
Rosa Parks	**Jackie Robinson**

segregation	boycott	discrimination
integration	desegregation	stereotypes

Name _____

 **Beyond the Borders of North Carolina**

Directions: Follow the directions in the order they appear below to complete the map on page 32. Write answers on the blanks provided.

1. **Label each state with its postal abbreviation.**

2. **Draw a star on the map to represent the location of each capital city. Then label each capital city on the map.**
   - _____ is the capital of West Virginia.
   - _____ is the capital of Virginia.
   - _____ is the capital of Kentucky.
   - _____ is the capital of Tennessee.
   - _____ is the capital of North Carolina.
   - _____ is the capital of South Carolina.
   - _____ is the capital of Arkansas.
   - _____ is the capital of Mississippi.
   - _____ is the capital of Alabama.
   - _____ is the capital of Georgia.
   - _____ is the capital of Louisiana.
   - _____ is the capital of Florida.

3. **Draw three brown triangles to represent the location of each mountain range. Then label each mountain range on the map.**
   - The _____ stretch from northern West Virginia and Virginia through northern Alabama and Georgia.
   - The _____ are located in northern Arkansas.

4. **Mark green X's to show where the following wetland area is located; then label the wetland area on the map.**
   - The _____ are located in the southern part of Florida.

5. **Use a blue marker or crayon to color or trace each body of water on the map. Then label the river or lake.**
   - Lake Pontchartrain is in southeastern _____.
   - Lake Okeechobee is in south central _____.
   - The Mississippi River forms the border between _____ and _____ and a portion of the border between _____ and _____.
   - The Mississippi Delta lies at the mouth of the Mississippi River in southern _____.
   - The Chattahoochee River flows from northern _____ through _____ and into the Gulf of Mexico.
   - The Ohio River forms the northwestern border of _____ and the northern border of _____.
   - The Roanoke River flows from _____ through _____.
   - Kentucky Lake lies across the border between _____ and _____.
   - The Savannah River forms the western border of _____.

6. **Lightly color each state according to the key below.**

Arkansas—orange	Georgia—red	Virginia—light blue
Louisiana—yellow	Florida—blue	West Virginia—dark green
Mississippi—light green	South Carolina—brown	Kentucky—purple
Alabama—pink	North Carolina—gray	Tennessee—tan

Name _____

The Southeast Region

Atlantic Ocean

Gulf of Mexico

PART 3: INDIVIDUAL REGIONAL PROJECTS

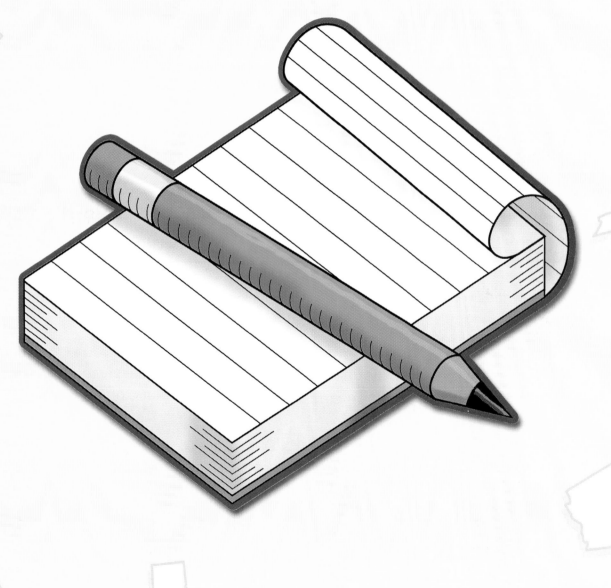

Name _____

Pick-a-Project

Group 1

- ☐ Make a poster highlighting some important vocabulary of the Southeast.

- ☐ Create a menu using food found in the Southeast.

- ☐ List the ages, locations, and names of the lighthouses found along the North Carolina coast.

- ☐ Write a newspaper article about a famous person from the Southeast.

- ☐ Make a bingo game using facts about the Southeast.

Group 2

- ☐ Write a story about Blackbeard and his adventures off the North Carolina coast.

- ☐ Write a review about the story "Grounded."

- ☐ Write diary entries about your life as a NASCAR® driver.

- ☐ Write a poem about the Southeast.

- ☐ Give a persuasive speech detailing why the Southeast is a great place to live.

Group 3

- ☐ Write ten questions you would have asked a person living in North Carolina during the Civil War.

- ☐ Summarize events leading up to the Wright brothers' first successful airplane flight.

- ☐ Explain how the town of Wilmington, North Carolina, might prepare for a hurricane.

- ☐ Make a timeline showing the important events in the history of the Lost Colony.

- ☐ Compare and contrast North Carolina with two other states in the Southeast.

Group 4

- ☐ Design a greeting card for people moving to the Southeast.

- ☐ Write and perform a commercial for the North Carolina Board of Tourism.

- ☐ Design a replica of the Cape Hatteras lighthouse.

- ☐ Write and illustrate a story about five hot spots in the Southeast.

- ☐ Create a song about a famous event in the Southeast's history.

Pick-a-Project Contract

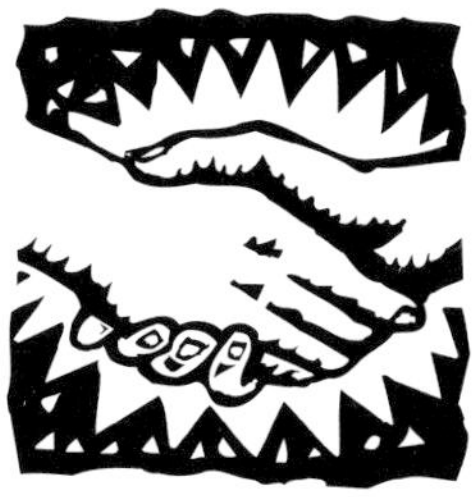

Name _____

Project _____

Due date _____

Materials/resources needed _____

_____

Plan for completing project _____

_____

_____

_____

Student signature _____ Teacher signature _____

Pick-a-Project Contract

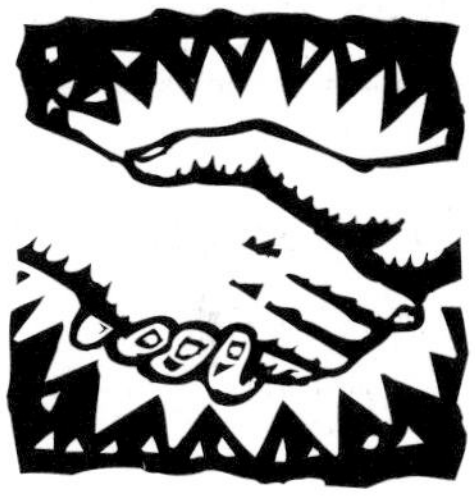

Name _____

Project _____

Due date _____

Materials/resources needed _____

_____

Plan for completing project _____

_____

_____

_____

Student signature _____ Teacher signature _____

Pick-a-Project Rubric

Name _____

	Project	Project	Project	Project
The contracted number of projects has been completed.	1 2 3 4 5	1 2 3 4 5	1 2 3 4 5	1 2 3 4 5
Each project has been turned in on time.	1 2 3 4 5	1 2 3 4 5	1 2 3 4 5	1 2 3 4 5
Each project has been completed according to the directions on page 34.	1 2 3 4 5	1 2 3 4 5	1 2 3 4 5	1 2 3 4 5
Each project is neat and pleasant to read.	1 2 3 4 5	1 2 3 4 5	1 2 3 4 5	1 2 3 4 5
Each project is well organized and easy to understand.	1 2 3 4 5	1 2 3 4 5	1 2 3 4 5	1 2 3 4 5
Each project has been proofread for spelling and punctuation, and any errors have been neatly corrected.	1 2 3 4 5	1 2 3 4 5	1 2 3 4 5	1 2 3 4 5
Each project contains accurate information about North Carolina or the Southeast.	1 2 3 4 5	1 2 3 4 5	1 2 3 4 5	1 2 3 4 5
Each project is creative and fun.	1 2 3 4 5	1 2 3 4 5	1 2 3 4 5	1 2 3 4 5
Final score:				

©2001 The Education Center, Inc. • Mystery States • Southeast Region • TEC3715

PART 4: MAPS & RESOURCES

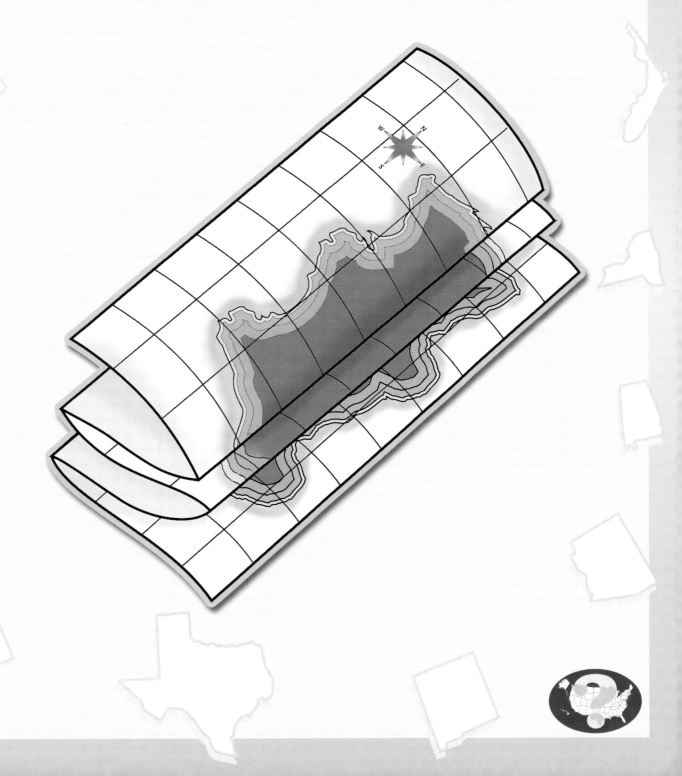

NORTH CAROLINA

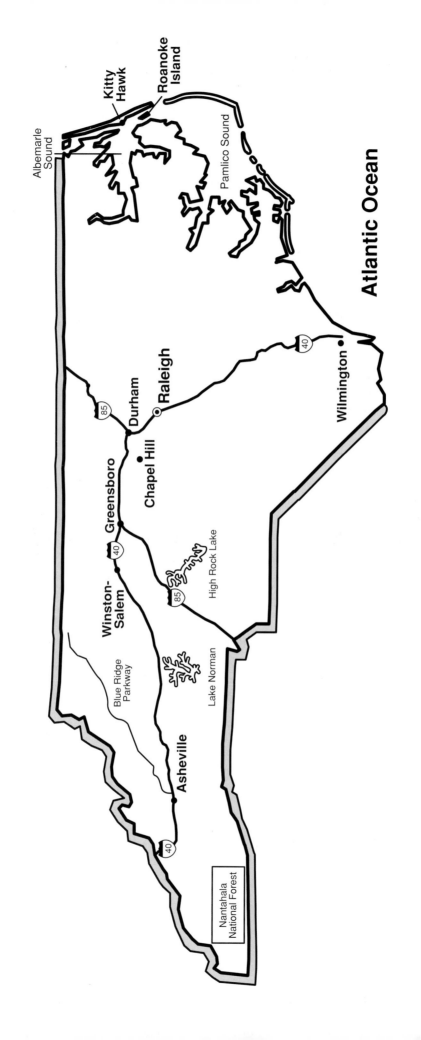

Kitty Hawk

Roanoke Island

Albemarle Sound

Pamlico Sound

Atlantic Ocean

Durham

Raleigh

Chapel Hill

Greensboro

85

40

Wilmington

40

Winston-Salem

High Rock Lake

Blue Ridge Parkway

85

Lake Norman

Asheville

40

Nantahala National Forest

THE SOUTHEAST STATES

Atlantic Ocean

Gulf of Mexico

THE UNITED STATES

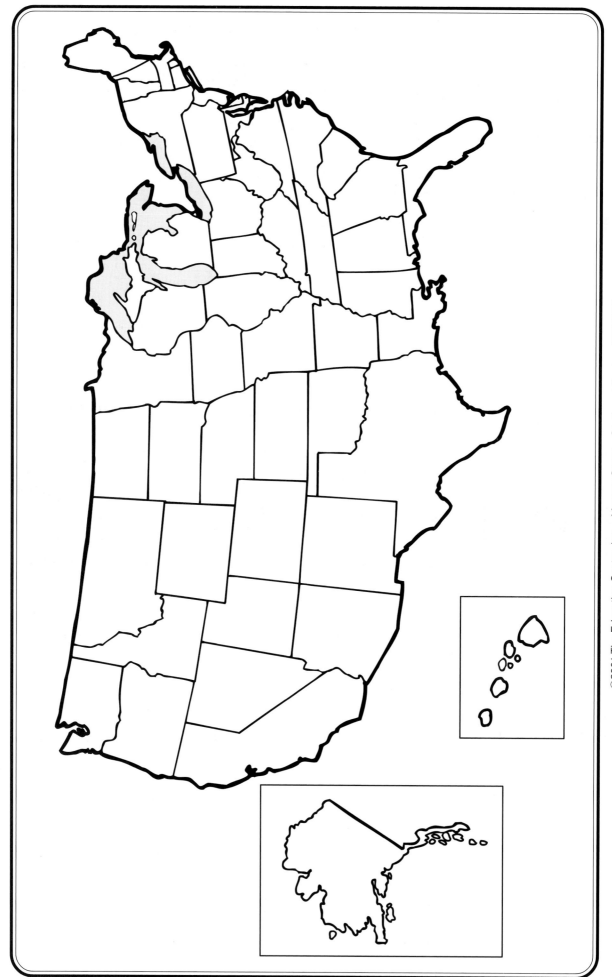

SYMBOLS OF NORTH CAROLINA

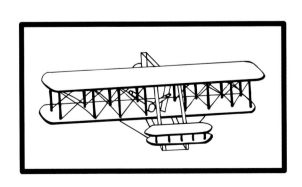

41

Resource Guide

Picture Books & Novels

Back Home by Gloria Jean Pinkney (Dial Books for Young Readers, 1992)

Burnin' Rubber: Behind the Scenes in Stock Car Racing by George Sullivan (The Millbrook Press, Inc.; 1998)

First Flight: The Story of Tom Tate and the Wright Brothers by George Shea (HarperCollins Children's Books, 1997)

Follow the Leader by Vicki Winslow (Bantam Books, Inc.; 1998)

An Island Scrapbook: Dawn to Dusk on a Barrier Island by Virginia Wright-Frierson (Simon & Schuster Books for Young Readers, 1998)

The Jack Tales by Richard Chase (Houghton Mifflin Company, 1993)

Littlejim's Gift: An Appalachian Christmas Story by Gloria Houston (PaperStar, 1998)

*The Lyon's Crown (The Lyon Saga series) by M.L. Stainer (Chicken Soup Press, Inc.; 2000)

*The Lyon's Cub (The Lyon Saga series) by M.L. Stainer (Chicken Soup Press, Inc.; 1998)

*The Lyon's Pride (The Lyon Saga series) by M.L. Stainer (Chicken Soup Press, Inc.; 1998)

*The Lyon's Roar (The Lyon Saga series) by M.L. Stainer (Chicken Soup Press, Inc.; 1997)

*The Lyon's Throne (The Lyon Saga series) by M.L. Stainer (Chicken Soup Press, Inc.; 1999)

My Home Is Over Jordan by Sandra Forrester (Puffin Books, 2000)

North Carolina: Facts and Symbols (The States and Their Symbols series) by Shelley Swanson Sateren (Bridgestone Books, 2000)

The Road to Freedom: A Story of the Reconstruction (Jamestown's American Portraits series) by Jabari Asim (Jamestown Publishing, 2000)

Teach's Light by Nell Wise Wechter (University of North Carolina Press, 1999)

Who Comes With Cannons? by Patricia Beatty (Greenwillow Books, 1992)

The Wright Brothers (Inventors series) by Paul Joseph (ABDO & Daughters, 1996)

* Novels about the Lost Colony

Reference Books

Hurricanes (Facts on File Dangerous Weather series) by Michael Allaby (Facts on File, Inc.; 1997)

Lighthouses of the Carolinas: A Short History and Guide by Terrance Zepke (Pineapple Press, Inc.; 1998)

Lower Atlantic: North Carolina, South Carolina (Discovering America series) by Thomas G. Aylesworth and Virginia L. Aylesworth (Chelsea House Publishing, 1995)

North Carolina (Portrait of America series) by Kathleen Thompson (Raintree Steck-Vaughn Publishers, 1996)

North Carolina (America the Beautiful series) by Martin Hintz, Stephen V. Hintz, and R. Conrad Stein (Children's Press, 1998)

North Carolina (From Sea to Shining Sea series) by Dennis Brindell Fradin (Children's Press, 1994)

Red Pepper Fudge and Blue Ribbon Biscuits: Favorite Recipes and Stories From North Carolina State Fair Winners by Amy T. Rogers (Down Home Press, 1995)

Scholastic Atlas of the United States by David Rubel (Scholastic, Inc.; 2000)

Web Sites

(Current as of September 2000)

http://www.secretary.state.nc.us/kidspg/homepage.asp— North Carolina Secretary of State Kids Page

http://www.state.me.us/sos/kids/links/statelinks.htm—other state kids' pages

http://www.nascar.com—official NASCAR® Page

http://www.carolinas.net/links/visitnc.html—North Carolina travel guide

http://www.outer-banks.com/lighthouses.cfm—North Carolina's lighthouses

http://www.highcountryhost.com—North Carolina mountains

http://www.nws.noaa.gov—National Weather Service

http://www.nhc.noaa.gov/index.html—National Hurricane Center

Contacts

North Carolina Department of Commerce
4301 Mail Service Center
Raleigh, NC 27699-4301

North Carolina Division of Tourism, Film, and Sports Development
4324 Mail Service Center
Raleigh, NC 27699-4324
(919) 733-4171

I-85 North Welcome Center
Box 156
Norlina, NC 27563
(252) 456-3236

PART 5:
ANSWER KEYS
& CHECKLIST

Answer Keys

Page 16

Clue 1
1. (17 states) Alabama, Connecticut, Illinois, Indiana, Kentucky, Maine, Massachusetts, Michigan, New Hampshire, New Jersey, New York, North Carolina, Ohio, South Carolina, Virginia, West Virginia, Wisconsin
2. (9 states) Connecticut, Maine, Massachusetts, New Hampshire, New Jersey, New York, North Carolina, South Carolina, Virginia

Clue 2
1. A hurricane is a powerful storm that measures 200–300 miles in diameter and has wind speeds above 73 miles per hour. A hurricane is an area of low air pressure that forms over the oceans of tropical regions in the North Atlantic Ocean and the eastern North Pacific Ocean.
2. (17 states) Alabama, Connecticut, Florida, Georgia, Louisiana, Maine, Maryland, Massachusetts, Mississippi, New Hampshire, New Jersey, New York, North Carolina, Rhode Island, South Carolina, Texas, Virginia
3. Florida, Louisiana, North Carolina, Texas

Clue 3
1. (12 states) Alabama, Connecticut, Georgia, Maine, Maryland, Massachusetts, New Hampshire, New Jersey, New York, North Carolina, South Carolina, Virginia
2. (6 states) Alabama, Georgia, Maryland, North Carolina, South Carolina, Virginia

Clue 4
1. (8 states) Alabama (Talladega Superspeedway), Delaware (Dover Downs International Speedway) Florida (Daytona International Speedway, Homestead-Miami Speedway), Georgia (Atlanta Motor Speedway), Kentucky (Louisville Motor Speedway, Kentucky Speedway), North Carolina (Lowe's Motor Speedway, North Carolina Speedway), South Carolina (Darlington Raceway, Myrtle Beach Speedway), Virginia (Martinsville Speedway, Richmond International Raceway, South Boston Speedway)
2. (7 states) Alabama, Delaware, Florida, Georgia, North Carolina, South Carolina, Virginia

Clue 5
1. (10 states) Alabama, Arizona, Arkansas, California, Georgia, Louisiana, Mississippi, North Carolina, Tennessee, Texas
2. (7 states) Alabama, Arkansas, Georgia, Louisiana, Mississippi, North Carolina, Tennessee
3. (5 states) Alabama, Georgia, Louisiana, Mississippi, North Carolina

Clue 6
1. (6 states) Georgia, Kentucky, North Carolina, South Carolina, Tennessee, Virginia
2. (4 states) Georgia, North Carolina, South Carolina, Virginia

Page 18
NORTH CAROLINA IS THE TAR HEEL STATE

Page 20
State Capital: Raleigh
State Tree: Pine
State Flower: Flowering dogwood
State Bird: Cardinal
(Answers will vary for the topics below. Possible answers are listed.)
Location
North Carolina is in the Southeast region of the United States. It is bordered by Virginia, the Atlantic Ocean, South Carolina, Georgia, and Tennessee.
Physical Land Features
North Carolina has three main land regions: the Atlantic Coastal Plain, the Piedmont, and the Mountain Region.
Natural Resources
North Carolina's main natural resources are rich soils, forests, and mineral deposits.
Climate & Weather
North Carolina has warm summers and mild to cold winters. Precipitation amounts vary by region.

Page 21
Answers will vary. Possible answers include the following:
Native Americans
The most important tribes living in North Carolina were the Catawba, Cherokee, Chowanoc, Hatteras, and Tuscarora.
History
1526—The Spanish tried unsuccessfully to set up a colony in North Carolina.
1585—The first English settlement was established on Roanoke Island.
1587—John White set up a new colony on Roanoke Island.
1590—White returned to find the colony deserted with no trace of the settlers. The colony became known as the Lost Colony.
1629—The land containing North Carolina and South Carolina was named the Province of Carolana after King Charles.
1765—The colonists began rebelling against British tax laws.
1774—Delegates from North Carolina were sent to the First Continental Congress in Philadelphia.
1789—North Carolina became the 12th state.
1861—North Carolina seceded from the Union.
1868—North Carolina abolished slavery.
1903—The Wright brothers were the first to successfully fly a powered airplane.
1950s and 1960s—Many black and white North Carolinians worked for civil rights.
Food
Foods produced or raised in North Carolina include chicken, corn, dairy products, fruit, peanuts, soybeans, sweet potatoes, and turkeys.
Famous People
Virginia Dare was born in Roanoke, North Carolina. She was the first English child born in North America.
Billy Graham is a well-respected television evangelist.
Jesse Jackson attended the Agricultural and Technical College of North Carolina. There he began fighting for civil rights.
Andrew Johnson was the 17th president of the United States.
Richard Petty is a NASCAR® national champion. He has had more victories than any other stock car driver.
Sugar Ray Leonard is the winner of several World Boxing Association and World Boxing Council championships.
Famous Landmarks
Biltmore Estate is located in Asheville. It has 250 rooms, making it the largest private house in the world.
Cape Hatteras Lighthouse stands about 208 feet above the ocean. It is the tallest brick lighthouse in the United States.
Grandfather Mountain is located along the Blue Ridge Parkway. At the mountain, tourists can walk across a mile-high swinging bridge.

Answer Keys

Page 22

Economy

North Carolina's primary industry is manufacturing. The state manufactures tobacco products, chemicals, textiles, machinery, electrical equipment, and food products. Jobs in education, health care, private research, and retail trade are also important parts of North Carolina's economy.

Inventions, Discoveries, & Firsts

1833—The first interstate railroad ran between Blakely, North Carolina, and Petersburg, Virginia.

1838—The first operating silver mine was opened near Lexington, North Carolina.

1898—Pepsi® cola was created in New Bern, North Carolina.

1903—The Wright brothers flew the first successful airplane at Kill Devil Hills, North Carolina.

1914—Babe Ruth hit his first professional home run in Fayetteville, North Carolina.

Places of Interest

Some tourist attractions in North Carolina include Alamance Battlefield, Biltmore Estate, Cherokee Indian Reservation, Chimney Rock, Nantahala Gorge, Ocracoke Island, and the U.S.S. *North Carolina* Battleship Memorial.

Plants

The Venus's-flytrap is only found growing in the wild in North Carolina and South Carolina. About two-thirds of North Carolina is forest. Some of the trees found in the state include pines, cypresses, hickories, maples, and oaks.

Animals

Some animals found in North Carolina include alligators, beavers, black bears, bobcats, deer, foxes, geese, gray squirrels, otters, raccoons, rattlesnakes, swans, and turtles.

Page 23

1. The Lost Colony was an English settlement established in 1587.
2. The colony was located on Roanoke Island, off the North Carolina coast.
3. The leader of the colony was John White.
4. The settlers came from England.
5. One hundred seventeen people settled the Lost Colony. Of these, 91 were men, 17 were women, and 9 were children.
6. Native Americans—including the Croatoan, or Hatteras, Indians—were living in the area when the settlers arrived.
7. John White left the colony in 1587 to return to England to gather more supplies.
8. John White's daughter Eleanor was important because she gave birth to Virginia Dare 27 days after the settlers arrived on Roanoke Island. The baby was the first English child born in America.
9. White returned to the Lost Colony in 1590. His return was delayed by the war between England and Spain.
10. When White reached the Lost Colony, he found it had been abandoned.
11. The settlers carved the letters *CRO* on one tree and the word *CROATOAN* on another.
12. Historians believe that some members of the Lost Colony may have moved to Chesapeake Bay where they were killed by Indians. They also believe that other settlers may have married into Indian tribes.

Page 26

Elizabeth Dole—Dole was born July 29, 1936, in Salisbury, North Carolina. Dole has worked for six different presidents. She has served as president of the American Red Cross.

William Sidney Porter—Porter was born near Greensboro, North Carolina, in 1862. He was well-known as the short story writer O. Henry.

Maya Angelou—Angelou was born in 1928. She moved to North Carolina in the early 1980s and is a professor at Wake Forest University. Angelou is a writer and poet. Her most famous book is *I Know Why the Caged Bird Sings.*

Andy Griffith—Griffith was born in Mount Airy, North Carolina, in 1926. The actor is famous for his roles in *The Andy Griffith Show* and *Matlock.*

Thelonious Monk—Monk was born October 10, 1917, in Rocky Mount, North Carolina. He was a pianist and composer. Monk was nominated for a Grammy in 1963.

Charles Kuralt—Kuralt was born in Wilmington, North Carolina, in 1934. As a journalist, he won the Emmy® and Peabody Awards. Kuralt was the host of CBS's *Sunday Morning.*

Answer Keys

Page 27

Dolley Madison—Madison was born in Piedmont, North Carolina, in 1768. She was the wife of President James Madison. She rescued George Washington's picture and many important documents from the White House when it was set on fire in 1814.

Richard Petty—Petty was born in Level Cross, North Carolina, in 1937. He began his professional auto racing career in 1958. Petty won the NASCAR® national championship and the Daytona 500 seven times each.

Michael Jordan—Jordan played basketball for the University of North Carolina and helped the team win an NCAA Division 1 championship in 1982. Jordan continued his basketball success by winning two gold medals at the Olympic® Games and 6 NBA championships with the Chicago Bulls®.

Mia Hamm—Hamm played soccer for the University of North Carolina and helped the team win several national championships.

Ava Gardner—Gardner was born in 1922 in Smithfield, North Carolina. She was an acclaimed actress, winning both Oscar® and Golden Globe nominations for her work.

Andrew Jackson—Jackson was born in western North Carolina in 1767. He was the seventh president of the United States.

Page 28

1. Hurricanes form over the ocean in tropical regions.
2. Hurricanes develop when sea temperatures reach at least 82°F.
3. A hurricane is a doughnut-shaped storm.
4. A calm *eye,* or center, is found in the middle of a hurricane.
5. A hurricane can have winds from 74 to 200 mph.
6. Moving over land causes hurricanes to weaken.
7. A hurricane's diameter can stretch 50–100 miles.
8. Meteorologists can forecast a hurricane's strength and predict its path.
9. Meteorologists can usually warn of an approaching hurricane several days in advance.
10. Hurricanes usually travel west or northwest at an average rate of 10 mph.

Page 29

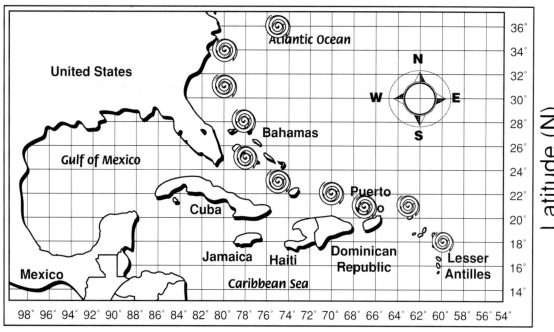

Longitude (W)

Page 31

1. Label each state with its postal abbreviation.

2. Draw a star on the map to represent the location of each capital city. Then label each capital city on the map.
    *   _Charleston_ is the capital of West Virginia.
    *   _Richmond_ is the capital of Virginia.
    *   _Frankfort_ is the capital of Kentucky.
    *   _Nashville_ is the capital of Tennessee.
    *   _Raleigh_ is the capital of North Carolina.
    *   _Columbia_ is the capital of South Carolina.
    *   _Little Rock_ is the capital of Arkansas.
    *   _Jackson_ is the capital of Mississippi.
    *   _Montgomery_ is the capital of Alabama.
    *   _Atlanta_ is the capital of Georgia.
    *   _Baton Rouge_ is the capital of Louisiana.
    *   _Tallahassee_ is the capital of Florida.

3. Draw three brown triangles to represent the location of each mountain range. Then label each mountain range on the map.
    *   The _Appalachian Mountains_ stretch from northern West Virginia and Virginia through northern Alabama and Georgia.
    *   The _Ozark Mountains_ are located in northern Arkansas.

4. Mark green X's to show where the following wetland area is located; then label the wetland area on the map.
    *   The _Everglades_ are located in the southern part of Florida.

5. Use a blue marker or crayon to color or trace each body of water on the map. Then label the river or lake.
    *   Lake Pontchartrain is in southeastern _Louisiana_ .
    *   Lake Okeechobee is in south central _Florida_ .
    *   The Mississippi River forms the border between _Arkansas_ and _Mississippi (or Tennessee)_ and a portion of the border between _Louisiana_ and _Mississippi_ .
    *   The Mississippi Delta lies at the mouth of the Mississippi River in southern _Louisiana_ .
    *   The Chattahoochee River flows from northern _Georgia_ through _Florida_ and into the Gulf of Mexico.
    *   The Ohio River forms the northwestern border of _West Virginia_ and the northern border of _Kentucky_ .
    *   The Roanoke River flows from _Virginia_ through _North Carolina_ .
    *   Kentucky Lake lies across the border between _Tennessee_ and _Kentucky_ .
    *   The Savannah River forms the western border of _South Carolina_ .

Page 32

Use the map to check the appropriate parts of problems 1–6 on page 31.
(Map shows approximate locations.)

Activity Checklist

Southeast	pp. 8–18	pp. 20–22	pp. 23–24	pp. 25–27	pp. 28–29	p. 30	pp. 31–32	pp. 34–36		
Student Names	Solved the Mystery State	Carolina on My Mind	Lost Colony	Guess Who	Hurricane Lab	Separate But Equal	Beyond the Borders of North Carolina	Pick-a-Project	Pick-a-Project Contract	Pick-a-Project Rubric